E
SIM
c.1

Simon, Norma

I know what I like

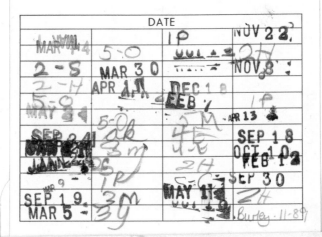

| DATE | | | |
|---|---|---|---|
| MAR 14 | 5-0 | 1P OCT | NOV 22 2H |
| 2-5 | MAR 30 | | NOV 8 |
| 2-H | APR 11 | DEC 18 | |
| 5-0 | | FEB | 1P |
| MAY 8 | 5-0 | 5M | APR 13 |
| SEP 24 | 2k 3m | 4E 4E | SEP 18 |
| JAN 21 | 6p | 2H | OCT 10a FEB 12 |
| SEP 19 | 1P 3M | MAY 11 | SEP 30 2H |
| MAR 5 | 3g | | Burley 11-89 |

HINES

By *Norma Simon*
ALL KINDS OF FAMILIES
CUANDO ME ENOJO...
HOW DO I FEEL?
I KNOW WHAT I LIKE
I WAS SO MAD!
WHAT DO I DO?
WHAT DO I DO? (English/Spanish edition)
WHAT DO I SAY?
WHAT DO I SAY? (English/Spanish edition)
WHY AM I DIFFERENT?
WE REMEMBER PHILIP

# I Know What I Like

NORMA SIMON

Pictures by DORA LEDER

ALBERT WHITMAN & Company
Chicago

*For Steffi, Wendy, and Jon*

**Simon, Norma.**
   I know what I like. Pictures by Dora Leder. A. Whitman [c1971].
   1 v. (unpaged) illus.
   Pictures and a simple text tell what children like and
don't like to do.

   1. Picture books for children.  I. Title.

X24201                          E
LJ Cards, c1971

Fourth Printing 1981
ISBN 0-8075-3507-9   L.C. Catalog Card 76-165822
Text ©1971 by Norma Simon     Illustrations ©1971 by Dora Leder
Published simultaneously in Canada by General Publishing, Limited, Toronto
Lithographed in U.S.A. All rights reserved.

*A Note About This Book*

EACH CHILD with whom you share this book, like each of the children in the story, is a unique, developing individual with feelings about what he likes and what he doesn't. When a child is encouraged to identify his likes and dislikes, to name them, list them, and talk about them, he grows in his own self-estimation and takes pleasure in claiming a particular preference.

Reactions to things, people, places, and experiences are continually changing. Responses are different for different children and change as children mature. With this book that specifically calls attention to preferences, an adult can help a child explore and gain insight into his reactions. The child can be encouraged to try out new feelings and to understand some ways in which his own likes and dislikes have changed as he himself has changed.

When a child becomes aware that other people do not necessarily like the same things he does, he gains respect and understanding for the preferences of others. Even more important, he learns that people can be friends even if they choose some very different things to like.

NORMA SIMON

**I** know what I like.
Do you know what you like?

I like to make pudding.

I like to make pictures.

I like to make faces.

But I don't like to make my bed
or pick up in my room.

(I do it anyway.)

I like to touch my toes.

I like to touch treetops.

I like to
touch a rabbit.

But I don't like to touch a hot stove
or *anything* too hot.

I like to be silly.

I like to be dressed up.

I like to be first in line.

But I don't like to be spanked.

Who does?

I like to smell cocoa.

I like to smell new shoes.

I like to smell flowers.

But I don't like to smell garbage.
*Yiiich!*

I like to
see the stars.

I like to see kittens.

I like to see myself.

I don't like
to see scary
television.

But maybe you do?

I like to hear bacon sizzle.

I like to hear a guitar.

I like to hear somebody
coming home.

But I don't like
to hear people yell—
especially when
I'm in bed.

I like to taste peanut butter.

I like to taste apple cider.

I like to taste toasted marshmallows.

But I don't like to taste this medicine.
(My daddy *says* he does.)

I like to catch a bus.

I like to catch a fish.

I like to catch a ball.

But I don't like to catch a cold.
It feels awful.

I like to try to guess.

I like to try new cookies.

I like
to try on hats.

But I don't like to try acting brave
when I have to get a shot.

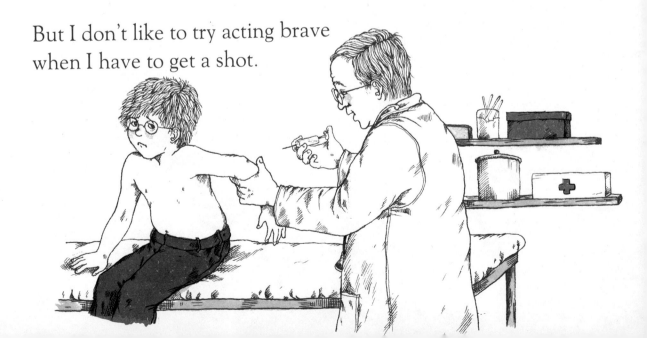

I like to play a drum.

I like to play with a puppy.

I like to play a game.

But I don't like
to play baby for my sister.

My sister likes it!

I like to go to the store.

I like to go
to Grandma's.

I like to go to my hiding place.

But I don't like to go to bed early.
(Grandma always does.)

You know what you like
and don't like.

I know what I like
and don't like.

I like being me.
I'm a boy— I like being a boy.

And I like being me.
I'm a girl— I like being a girl.

Everybody likes friends,
and we all like to be friends.

*About the Author*

Norma Simon grew up in New York City—in Brooklyn, the Bronx, and Manhattan—but she and her husband, Edward Simon, and their children prefer a Cape Cod home where life seems to retain a more balanced reality.

When she was a little girl, Norma Simon liked roller skating and jumping rope. She enjoyed reading as many of the books as she could find on the children's shelves in her neighborhood branch library. She herself became a children's author when her first book appeared in 1954. It has been followed by almost thirty others, mostly for young children, but including one semi-autobiographical story for girls.

Norma Simon did her undergraduate work at Brooklyn College and then obtained an M.S. from the Bank Street College of Education in New York City. She is on the Bank Street staff as an educational consultant and has worked with emotionally disturbed children in child guidance centers in Norwalk and Bridgeport, Connecticut. A long career in preschool teaching and more recently in planning Headstart programs has made Mrs. Simon especially aware of the need for books that deal realistically with everyday life. Her What Do I Say? and What Do I Do? were written with this need in mind and are available in both English and English with Spanish.

*Norma Simon is a member of the Authors Guild*